CONTENTS

CAST LIST

NARRATORS	We've split this role into 4 manageable parts, but you can use more or less as you wish – or if preferred, an adult.
EDDIE	Suited to an older, more confident child. Quite a few short lines to deliver.
THE PENGUIN FAMILY:	
MOTHER	
GRANNY	
GRANDPA	Use as many family members as you need but these are the ones with spoken lines in the script.
UNCLE	
AUNTY	
CHICKS	
PEGGY POLAR BEAR	She's the leader of the pack when it comes to polar bears!
POLAR BEARS X 3	3 more bears with one short line each.
MR BOOT	A family man with a family car! One short line to remember.
SAM	Mr Boot's son – joins his dad with same spoken line.
MRS MOTOR	She likes her car too. One line to learn.
PAM	Mrs Motor's daughter – joins her mum with same spoken line.
3 CHILDREN	Great at walking, skipping and cycling to school – and telling us about it!
DJ DONNIE	A cool dude, with one simple line.
2 LUMBERJACKS	They're a bit too keen on cutting down trees – one simple line each.
PRIME MINISTER	Needs a bit of authority to deliver his/her one line.

You can add as many other non-speaking parts as suits, or combine some of the above to reduce the number of characters if required.

STAGING

There are many ways you could design your stage, depending on the size of your cast and the area you have to use. One idea would be to have a different zone for each country to be visited, so Eddie and the penguins would travel between these throughout the musical. Otherwise, a different backdrop or a direction sign to each country would show you've moved to a different location.

To the side of the stage, a large globe or picture of Earth would be good, with a child (or penguin) pointing to where Eddie is heading next.

IDEAS FOR EXTENSION WORK

SONG 1 THE MELTING SONG

Why not make a fact file about penguins, finding out where they live, their habitat requirements, what they eat and the sorts of things they like to do? Can anyone find out why they are black on their backs and white on their tummies?

Talk about ice – what it is and the importance of temperature. Can we make it? Can it float? Has anyone been ice-skating? What was it like?

Introduce the subject of biodiversity – the variety of plants and wildlife in the world around us. Talk about why it is important for us to protect our world and it's natural habitats, keeping vital links between living creatures and their environment.

SONG 2 WE'RE GREAT BIG POLAR BEARS

You could make another fact file about polar bears and compare the similarities and differences to penguins.

Polar bears like to swim. What other animals like to swim? Look at some pictures of animals that swim and describe how they are designed to move efficiently in water.

Could you have a polar bear as a pet? What other animals couldn't you have as pets? Talk about animals that make good pets and any pets the children have themselves.

SONG 3/4 THE WALKING SONG

Do any of the children walk to school? Apart from helping to cut down on pollution from cars, why else do the children think it is good to walk to school? (Can help keep you fit, you will be more alert in class, have time to talk, lots to see on the way, etc.)

Make a graph showing the different ways all the members of the class get to school. Which is the most popular?

Talk about types of transport, other than those mentioned in the song, that can be used to help save energy: buses, trains, trams. If the school doesn't already have one, why not set up a 'walk to school' scheme with the help of the local council to enable more children to take part; or develop a car-sharing scheme for those who live further away.

SONG 5 IF YOU'RE FEELING COOL, DRESS HOT!

Talk about energy and the sorts of appliances we use around the house that use up energy. The song mentions some ways to save energy. How else can we and our families try to conserve energy? (Turn down the central heating thermostat; wash clothes on a lower temperature; insulate lofts; have double glazing; use energy efficient light bulbs; don't leave TVs on standby; turn mobile phone chargers off when not in use, employ solar power, etc.)

SONG 6 TREES

Discuss the names of different trees and bring leaves into the classroom to identify. Look at the different parts of a tree; ie, leaf, root, branch, twig, trunk, bark, fruit and seeds. Produce a collage using the leaves, make leaf prints and have a go at some bark rubbings.

What do trees need to survive? Why are they good for our environment? (Trees turn carbon dioxide into oxygen which we need to breathe. This also helps reduce the amount of carbon dioxide that enters the atmosphere, making the earth too warm.)

Trees also help prevent soil erosion, and give wildlife such as squirrels, minibeasts and birds a place to live.

SONG 7 THE RECYCLING SONG

Make a list of all the things that can be recycled. (Glass bottles & jars, empty aerosol cans, plastic bottles, paper, cardboard, aluminium cans, paper bags, aluminium foil, foil trays, shredded paper, newspapers, phone books, frozen food boxes, mail, magazines, catalogues…)

If the children bring packed lunches to school, why not set up a recycling scheme for all the lunchtime waste? Create different collection bins to separate the cartons, foil, plastic bottles, paper, etc. You could also introduce a compost bin to compost any left-over fruit and veg and use this on the school garden. Perhaps devise a reward scheme with points for the child with the least waste each day/week/month.

SONG 8 ONE WORLD

Study a globe and look at pictures of the world. Appreciate that Earth is a sphere. Is it the only planet? What other planets are known? Where are they in relation to Earth and Sun? What would be found on the other planets? Are there any animals or trees? Why not? Make a wall collage of the planets showing their position, size and characteristics.

SONG 9 TURN OFF THE TAP!

Why should we save water? Talk about the fact that although there is plenty of water on the planet, it takes a lot of energy to collect and make clean enough for us to drink. The energy used adds to the greenhouse gases.

What do we use water for? List some of the main categories (gardening, bathing, flushing the toilet, cleaning teeth, washing hands). Using this list, each child could monitor how many times they, as individuals, use water for each category in one day. Discuss the results.

Talk about countries where water isn't so easily available and the problems this can cause. Can we do anything to help these countries?

SONG 10 USE IT AGAIN

Make some interesting things out of old CDs, clothes and other unwanted 'junk' materials. Get the children to use their imagination to make things that they otherwise would have bought new. Here are some ideas:

- an old crisp tube or play dough pot can make a money box
- reuse ice-lolly sticks as plant labels
- make gift tags out of pictures on used greetings cards
- make newspaper hats – paint and decorate them
- use throw away paper, labels, scraps cut from junk mail, anything you can find that is typically thrown away - to make a collage

Make simple musical instruments from empty bottles, cereal boxes, yoghurt pots and plastic cartons:

- make shakers by putting dried rice or pasta into a yoghurt pot then sealing a second pot onto the filled one, or by filling plastic bottles with sand or beads
- use a stick and a ridged plastic bottle to make a scraper
- a guitar can be made by stretching elastic bands over an empty tissue box or plastic pipe
- fill glass bottles with different levels of water and blow across them to make sounds, or tap them with a metal object (eg spoon) to make them ring
- decorate the instruments with coloured paper and glitter

SCRIPT & SONG LYRICS

NARRATOR 1	Deep in Antarctica, under the cold, cold sky, Eddie the penguin was thinking. He thought about the beautiful world he lived in and he thought about his family.
NARRATOR 2	Eddie had an enormous family. There was his wife, Mother Penguin…
MOTHER PENGUIN	Hello!
NARRATOR 2	Granny Penguin…
GRANNY PENGUIN	Hello!
NARRATOR 2	Grandpa Penguin…
GRANDPA PENGUIN	Hello!
NARRATOR 2	Aunty Penguin…
AUNTY PENGUIN	Hello!
NARRATOR 2	Uncle Penguin…
UNCLE PENGUIN	Hello!
NARRATOR 2	And lots of penguin chicks…
PENGUIN CHICKS	Hello!
NARRATOR 1	They all liked to have lots of fun.

If preferred, the following 6 lines could be given to individual penguin chicks to create more speaking parts.

MOTHER PENGUIN	Swimming!
GRANNY PENGUIN	Diving!
UNCLE PENGUIN	Eating fish!
GRANDPA PENGUIN	Riding on the icebergs!
AUNTY PENGUIN	Flip, flip, flapping!
PENGUIN CHICKS	Sliding!
NARRATOR 1	One day when Eddie Penguin was having a rest on the ice, he noticed something very strange. He could hear a sound. It went drip, drop, drip, drop, drip, drop. What could it be?
NARRATOR 3	As he looked, he saw that the ice was melting and melting away. He called to his family.

EDDIE The ice is melting, the ice is melting!

EVERYONE Oh no, the ice is melting!!!

Song 1. THE MELTING SONG

1 Drip, drop, can you hear a sound?
Drip, drop, drip, drop.
Drip, drop, can you hear a sound?
Drip, drop, drip, drop.
The icebergs where we like to play
Are melting, melting away,
Drip, drop, drip, drop, drip, drop.

2 Drip, drop, can you hear a sound?
Drip, drop, drip, drop.
Drip, drop, can you hear a sound?
Drip, drop, drip, drop.
The snowy hills where we like to slide
Are melting in front of our eyes,
Drip, drop, drip, drop, drip, drop.

3 Drip, drop, can you hear a sound?
Drip, drop, drip, drop.
Drip, drop, can you hear a sound?
Drip, drop, drip, drop.
The icy land where we like to meet
Is melting under our feet,
Drip, drop, drip, drop, drip, drop.
Drip, drop, drip, drop, drip, drop.

NARRATOR 2 What could the penguins do? Where could they find more ice? Eddie thought for a while, then he said…

EDDIE I know what to do!

NARRATOR 1 Eddie the Penguin decided that he and his family should go on a journey to find a new home. He gathered everyone around him and they all agreed with Eddie that they would have to travel right to the other side of the world.

NARRATOR 2 The very next day, the penguins set off on a very long journey, all the way to the North Pole, to see if there was any more ice there.

NARRATOR 3 They travelled for months and months. They rode on a whale over the sea; they marched and marched over the land until finally they got to the North Pole. Will there be any more ice here, they wondered?

NARRATOR 4 As they looked around, they could see something in the distance. They walked closer and closer - it was a big white animal.

PEGGY POLAR BEAR Hello, I'm Peggy Polar Bear.

NARRATOR 1 Peggy Polar Bear looked very fed up. Then more polar bears appeared and they looked fed up too.

EDDIE What's the matter?

POLAR BEAR 2 The ice is melting.

Song 2. WE'RE GREAT BIG POLAR BEARS

1 We're great big polar bears sitting on the ice
And we all think that ice is nice.
We're great big polar bears sitting on the ice
And we all think that ice is nice.

CHORUS *Don't let the ice,*
Don't let the ice,
Don't let the ice melt away.

2 It's getting warmer and we're feeling hot,
All this melting has to stop.
It's getting warmer and we're feeling hot,
All this melting has to stop.

CHORUS

3 We're great big polar bears sitting on the ice
And we all think that ice is nice.
We're great big polar bears sitting on the ice
And we all think that ice is nice!

NARRATOR 2 So the ice was melting at the North Pole too. Eddie wondered why this was happening. He asked the polar bears if they knew why.

POLAR BEAR 3 It's the human beings.

POLAR BEAR 4 They are making our planet too hot.

NARRATOR 3 This made Eddie very worried. He decided that they should go and see the human beings. So they set off on another journey, all the way to the United Kingdom.

NARRATOR 4 When they got to the UK, the penguins couldn't believe their eyes. There were enormous cars everywhere! Vroom, vroom – the enormous noisy cars used up lots of energy. The pollution from their exhausts went up into the sky and made the earth warmer and warmer.

NARRATOR 1 The penguins came to a school. Along came Mr Boot and his son Sam, in their great big car.

MR BOOT & SAM Vroom, vroom, we like driving!

NARRATOR 1 Then came Mrs Motor and her daughter Pam.

MRS MOTOR & PAM Vroom, vroom, we like driving!

NARRATOR 2 More and more cars arrived at the school and soon, there were lots of people at the school gates.

NARRATOR 3 Then Eddie had an idea. He whispered to the other penguins and they all started to sing.

Song 3. THE WALKING SONG

1 If your journey's short you could walk to school,
Walking can be really cool.
It can make you fit,
Have you thought about it?
You could walk, walk to school.

2 If your journey's short you could skip to school,
Skipping can be really cool.
It can make you fit,
Have you thought about it?
You could skip, skip to school.

3 If your journey's short you could scooter to school,
Scooting can be really cool.
It can make you fit,
Have you thought about it?
You could scoot, scoot to school.

4 If your journey's short you could cycle to school,
Cycling can be really cool.
It can make you fit,
Have you thought about it?
You could cycle, cycle to school.

CHILD 1 We can walk to school!

CHILD 2 We can skip to school!

CHILD 3 We can cycle to school!

NARRATOR 4 The mums and dads and children thought this was a very good idea and they all joined in with the song.

Song 4. THE WALKING SONG (Reprise – verses 1 & 2)
(Children could hold up lyrics for the audience to sing along)

NARRATOR 1 Then every day after that, the children started walking and skipping to school. Some people travelled by bus, some people travelled by train, and the planet started to cool down.

NARRATOR 2 Eddie and his penguins continued their journey. They went all the way to America. When they got there, they could see lots of houses. Lights streamed from every window; tumble dryers went round and round; everyone had their heating turned up high and left all the doors open. All the greenhouse gasses produced from using all this energy went up into the sky and made the earth warmer and warmer.

GRANNY PENGUIN What can we do?

NARRATOR 3 Eddie took all the penguins to a radio station and there, they met DJ Donnie.

EDDIE We've got an important message for everyone. Can we go on air?

NARRATOR 3 So DJ Donnie spoke into his microphone.

DJ DONNIE *(Loudly)* And tonight, we have live, Eddie and the penguins!

Song 5. IF YOU'RE FEELING COOL, DRESS HOT!

1 If you're feeling cool today, dress hot, dress hot,
If you're feeling cool today, dress hot, dress hot.
You can save some energy,
This is how we want to be,
So if you're feeling cool, dress hot!

2 If the weather's fine then hang your washing on the line,
If the weather's fine then hang your washing on the line.
You can save some energy,
This is how we want to be,
So if the weather's fine, use the line!

3 When you leave the room, don't forget, turn out the lights,
When you leave the room, don't forget, turn out the lights.
You can save some energy,
This is how we want to be,
So when you leave the room turn out the lights!

4 If you want to keep all the heat then shut that door,
If you want to keep all the heat then shut that door.
You can save some energy,
This is how we want to be,
So keep the heat and shut that door!

NARRATOR 4 So everyone started to dry their washing on a line, they turned the heating down and wore some warmer clothes. They remembered to turn off the lights and keep the doors shut and the planet cooled down a bit more.

NARRATOR 2 Off went Eddie and his family again. They marched for miles and miles, all the way to Brazil. They got on a boat and floated down the Amazon river, through the rain forest. But in the rain forest there were lots of people chopping all the trees down… every single one!

LUMBERJACK 1 Chop, chop, chop!

LUMBERJACK 2 We're chopping the trees down!

NARRATOR 3 And for every tree that was chopped down, the earth got warmer and warmer. The penguins called to the lumberjacks and all the people around…

EDDIE Listen to us, we will sing you a song!

Song 6. TREES

1 Beautiful trees standing high,
Reaching, reaching up to the sky.
Swallowing up the CO_2,
If we didn't have them, what would we do?
What would we do?

2 Swaying free in the breeze,
Bending branches, whispering leaves.
Keeping Earth cool as it goes round,
Please don't chop too many trees down,
Too many trees down.

3 Beautiful trees standing high,
Reaching, reaching up to the sky.
Swallowing up the CO_2,
If we didn't have them, what would we do?
What would we do?

NARRATOR 4 The people in Brazil listened to Eddie and the penguins. They stopped cutting down so many trees and started to plant extra trees instead. The planet cooled down a bit more.

NARRATOR 1 The penguins had one more place to go. They rode on their whale again, all the way to Australia. They marched on and on through the cities and as they went, they saw that everyone's bin was very full. The refuse collectors came to take all the rubbish away to a big landfill site. The landfill site was very smelly. Lots of gasses came out of the rubbish and went up into the sky, making the earth warmer and warmer… and it smelt awful!

GRANDPA PENGUIN We've got to do something about this!

NARRATOR 2 But Eddie had already decided what to do.

EDDIE Follow me!

NARRATOR 2 The penguins followed Eddie all the way to the city of Canberra and to a big house where the Prime Minister lived. Eddie wanted to teach the Prime Minister a special song that he could then sing to all the people. Eddie knocked at the door.

PRIME MINISTER I am the Prime Minister. What do you want?

EDDIE Mr Prime Minister, we want to teach you a song.

NARRATOR 2 So the penguins started to sing.

Song 7. THE RECYCLING SONG

1 Don't put your glass bottles in the trash,
Put them in a box, you can do it in a flash.
A lorry will take them, shine or rain,
Then we'll grind them up and use them again.

2 Don't put your cardboard in the trash,
Put it in a box, you can do it in a flash.
A lorry will take it, shine or rain,
Then we'll grind it up and use it again.

3 Don't put your paper in the trash,
Put it in a box, you can do it in a flash.
A lorry will take it, shine or rain,
Then we'll grind it up and use it again.

4 Don't put your plastics in the trash,
Put them in a box, you can do it in a flash.
A lorry will take them, shine or rain,
Then we'll grind them up and use them again.

5 Don't put your tin cans in the trash,
Put them in a box, you can do it in a flash.
A lorry will take them, shine or rain,
Then we'll grind them up and use them again.

NARRATOR 3 The Prime Minister thought that this was a very good song. He took all his ministers to a big television station where together they sang the song to the whole country.

(An optional reprise of The Recycling Song, with everyone singing, would work well here if time allows.)

NARRATOR 4 And from that day, every person in Australia recycled everything they could and the earth cooled down even more. It got icier in Antarctica, it got icier at the North Pole and in all the places where ice was needed.

NARRATOR 1 The polar bears shouted…

POLAR BEARS Our ice is back!

NARRATOR 1 The penguins shouted…

PENGUINS The ice is here again!

NARRATOR 1 And everyone on the planet shouted…

EVERYONE Well done Eddie and the penguins!!

Song 8. ONE WORLD

1 Think, think, think as you go, go, go,
Think, think, think, 'cos you know, know, know…

CHORUS *We have one world to care for*
So we must make sure
We think about our world today.

2 Think, think, think as you walk about,
Think, think, think as you shout it out…

CHORUS

3 Think, think, think every night and day,
Think, think, think, there's a better way.

CHORUS x 2

THE MELTING SONG

Words and Music by
Niki Davies

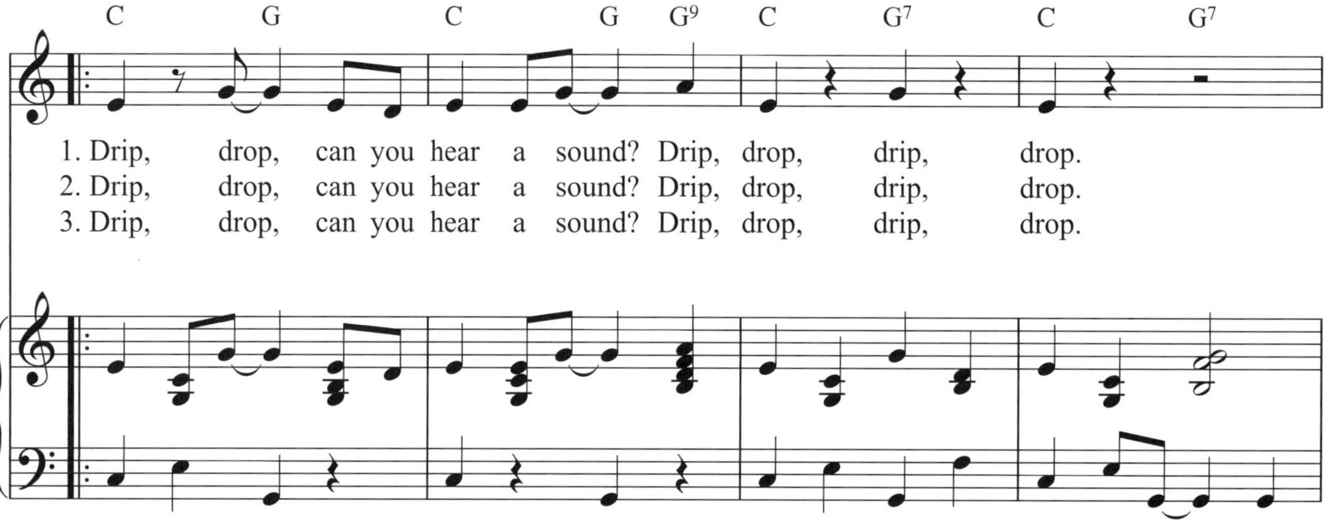

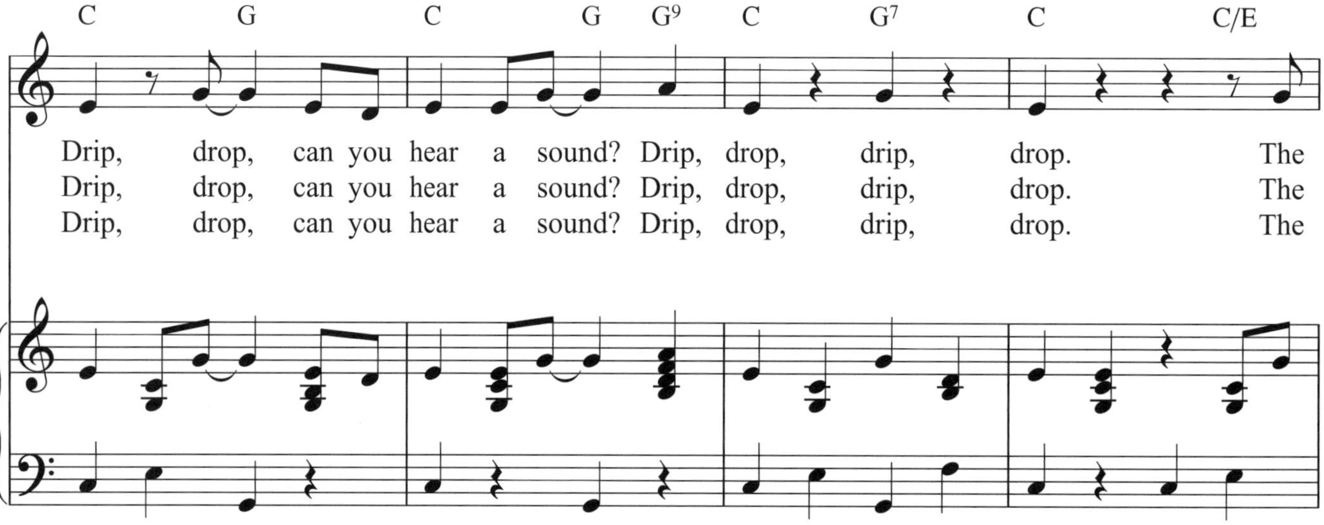

Dm7 Dm7/A G9 G7/B C C/B C/B♭ A7 A7/C♯
ice-bergs where we like to play_ are melt-ing, melt-ing a-way. Drip,
snow-y hills where we like to slide_ are melt-ing in front of our eyes. Drip,
i-cy land where we like to meet_ is melt-ing un-der our feet. Drip,
1. 2.
3.
Dm7 Dm9/A G7 G7+6 C G C G7 C C/B C/B♭
drop, drip, drop, drip, drop. drop.
drop, drip, drop, drip, drop.
drop, drip, drop, drip,
3
A7 A7/C♯ Dm7 Dm9/A G7 G7+6 C G7 C
Drip, drop, drip, drop, drip, drop.

We're Great Big Polar Bears

Words and Music by
Niki Davies

Moderately ♩ = 114

To Coda
Em Bm7 Am7 Bm7 Em Am9 D6 Am9 D6
we all think that ice is nice.
all this melt - ing has to stop.
Don't let the ice, don't let the ice,
Am9 D6 Em7 Bm7 Em Bm7 Am7 Bm7
don't let the ice melt a - way.
1. 2. D.S. al Coda
CODA
Em Bm7 Em Bm7 Am7 Bm7 Em Em2
2. It's
3. We're
ice is nice.
Ped.

THE WALKING SONG

Words and Music by
Niki Davies

F♯7 F♯7/E F♯7/C♯ F♯7 Bm7 E7 A Amaj7/E
thought a-bout it? You could walk, walk to school.
thought a-bout it? You could skip, skip to school.
thought a-bout it? You could scoot, scoot to school.
thought a-bout it? You could cy-cle, cy-cle to school.
1. 2. 3.
Bm7 E7 A Amaj7/E Bm7 E7
2. If your
3. If your
4. If your
4.
A Amaj7 Bm7 E7 A E7 A

THE WALKING SONG

(Reprise)

Words and Music by
Niki Davies

F♯7 F♯7/E F♯7/C♯ F♯7 Bm7 E7 A Amaj7/E
thought a-bout it? You could walk, walk to school.
thought a-bout it? You could skip, skip to school.
1.
Bm7 E7 A Amaj7/E Bm7 E7
2. If your
2.
A Amaj7 Bm7 E7 A E7 A

IF YOU'RE FEELING COOL, DRESS HOT!

Words and Music by
Niki Davies

With a swing 𝅗𝅥 = 98 (♩♪ = ♩ ♪ triplet)

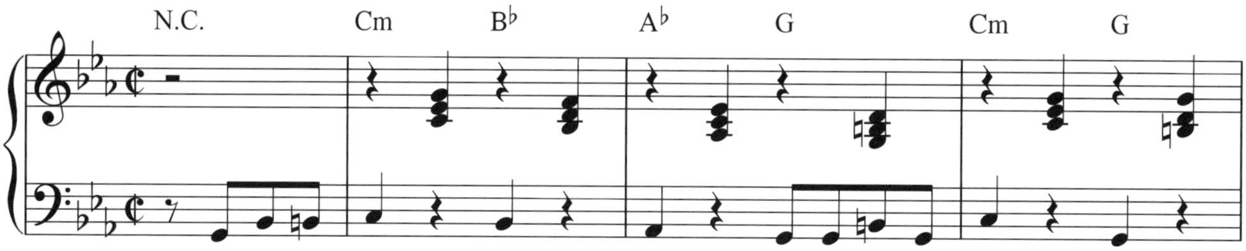

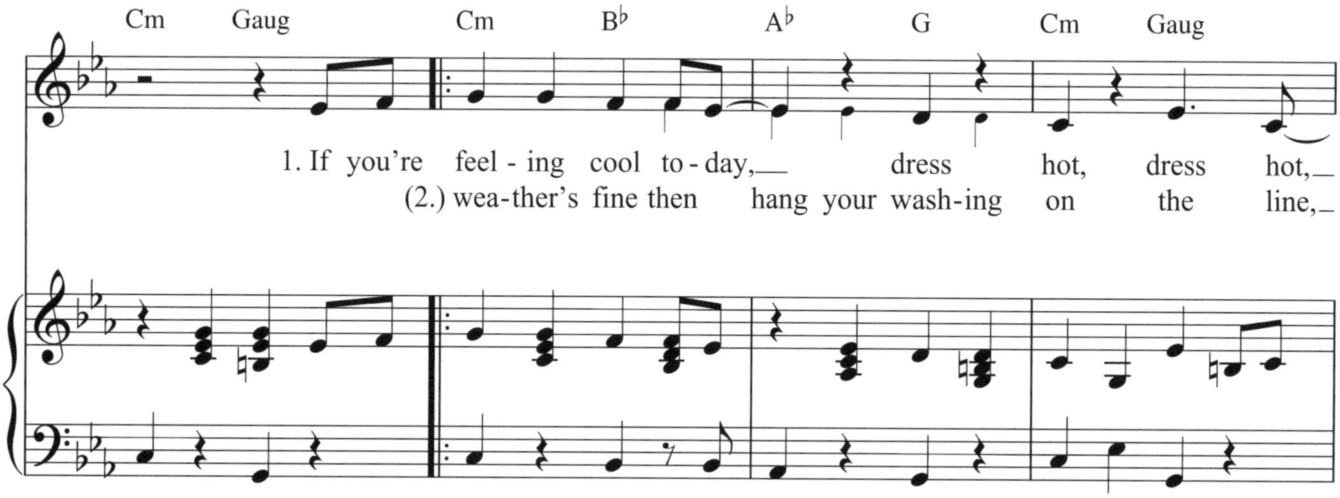

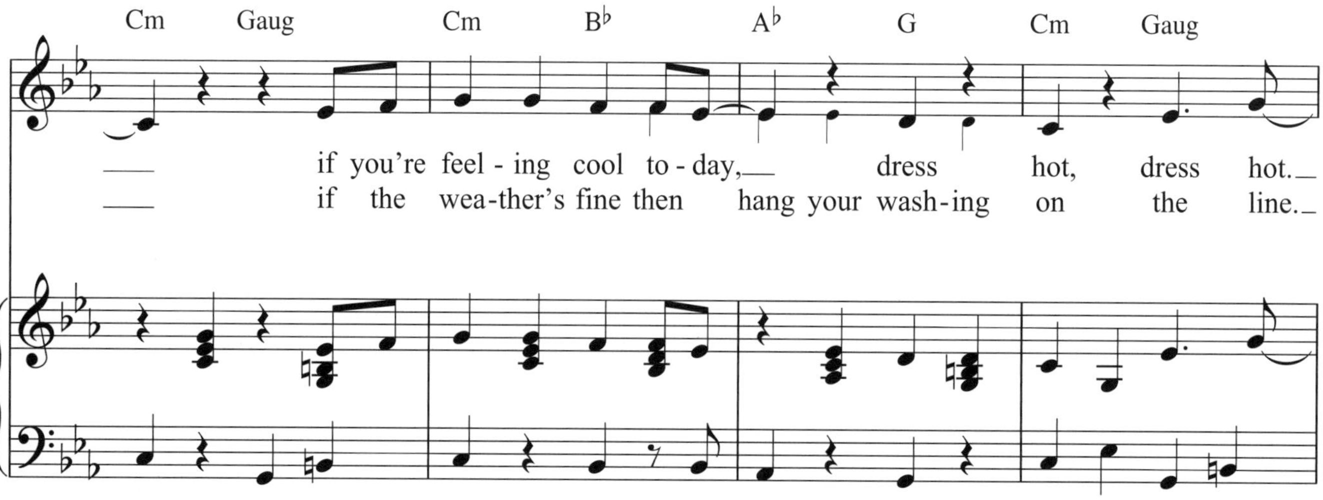

Cm C Dm7 C/E Fm7 Fm7/A♭ B♭7 B♭7/C B♭7/D E♭maj7 Emaj7/G Emaj7/B♭
You can save some en - er - gy, this is how we
You can save some en - er - gy, this is how we
Cm Cm/G Cm/E♭ Csus4 G Fm/G Cm/G Gm/B♭ Cm B♭
want to be, so if you're feel - ing cool, dress hot!
want to be, so if the wea-ther's fine, use the line!
1.
2.
A♭ G Cm G Cm Gaug Cm Gaug
2. If the
3. When you

Cm B♭ A♭ G Cm Gaug
leave the room, don't for - get,__ turn out the lights,_
(4.) want to keep all the heat__ then shut that door,__
Cm Gaug Cm B♭ A♭ G
when you leave the room, don't for - get,__ turn
if you want to keep all the heat__ then
Cm Gaug Cm C Dm7 C/E Fm7 Fm7/A♭
out the lights.__ You can save some
shut that door.__ You can save some

B♭7 B♭7/C B♭7/D E♭maj7 E♭maj7/G Emaj7/B♭ Cm Cm/G Cm/E♭ Csus4
en - er - gy, this is how we want to be, so
en - er - gy, this is how we want to be, so
G Fm/G Cm/G Gm/B♭ Cm B♭
when you leave the room turn out the lights!
keep the heat and shut that door!
1. 2.
A♭ G Cm G Cm Gaug Cm
4. If you
3

Trees

Words and Music by
Niki Davies

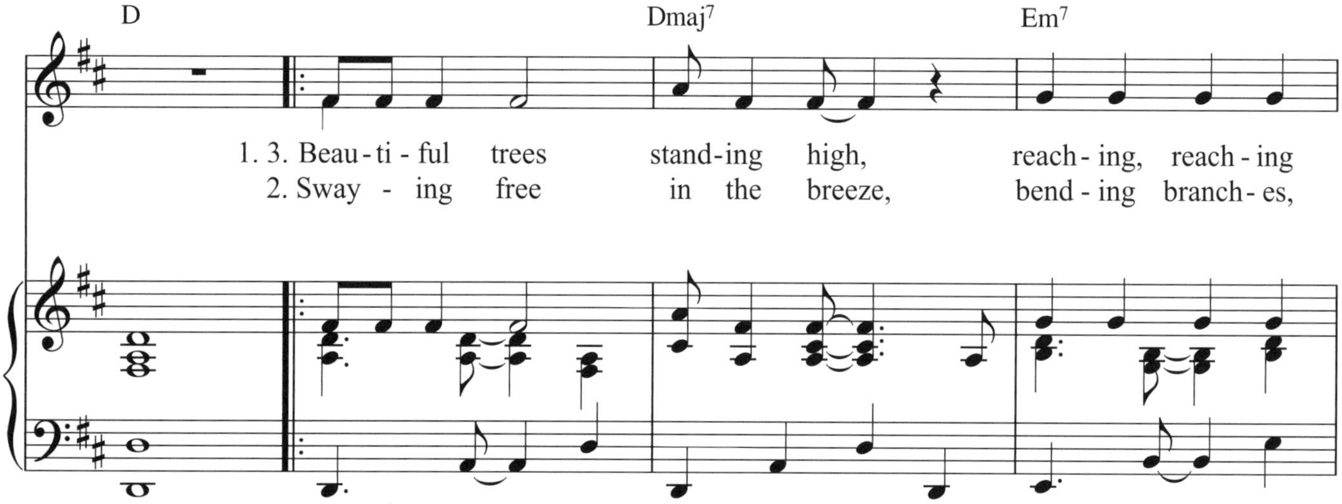

Em7
A7
Dmaj7
we did - n't have them, what would we do?
please don't chop too ma - ny trees down,
D9
A11
A
A7
1. 2.
D
What would we do?
too ma - ny trees down.
Dmaj7
Em7
A7
D
3.
D
Dmaj7
do?
rit.
Em7
A11
Em7
A7
D

THE RECYCLING SONG

Words and Music by
Niki Davies

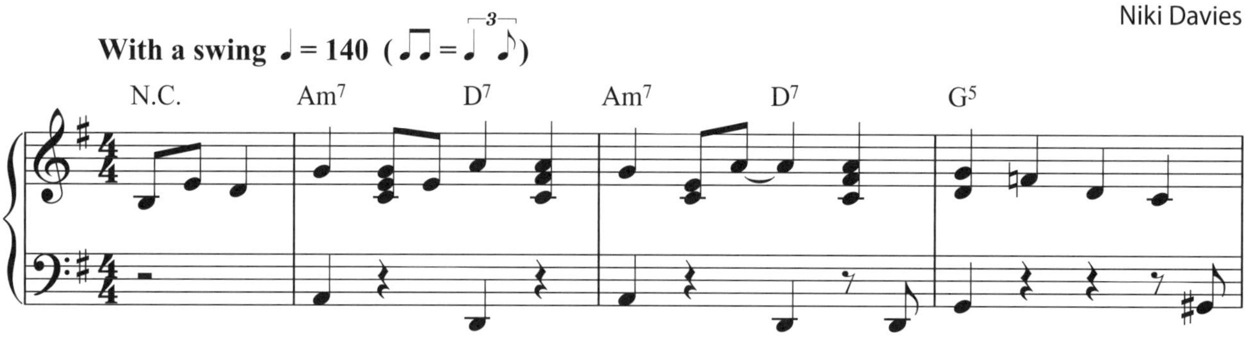

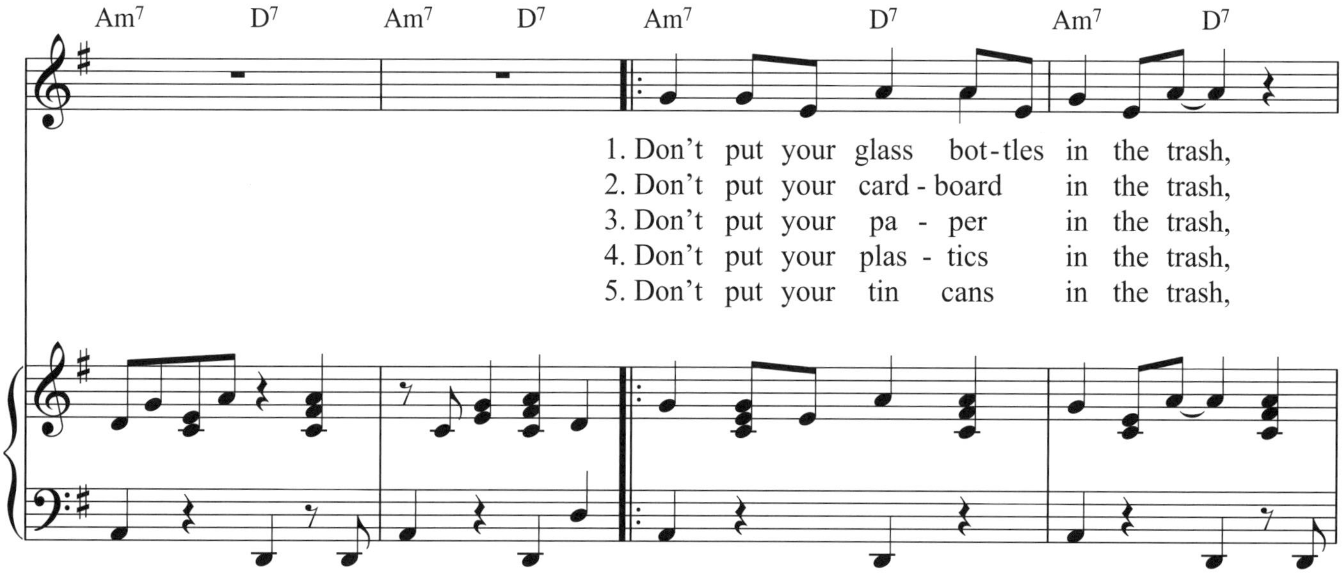

G F G5
shine or rain,_ then we'll grind them up and use them a - gain._
shine or rain,_ then we'll grind it up and use it a - gain._
shine or rain,_ then we'll grind it up and use it a - gain._
shine or rain,_ then we'll grind them up and use them a - gain._
shine or rain,_ then we'll grind them up and use them a - gain._
1 – 4.
Am7sus4 D7 Am7 D7 Am9 D7 Am7 D7
5.
Am7 D7 Am7 D7 G5 F5 D5 N.C. F5 G5

ONE WORLD

Words and Music by
Niki Davies

Am9 D Am9 D G9 G/B /B♭ A7
one world to care for_ so we_ must make sure_ we
To Coda
1. 2.
Am9 Am7 C/D D7 G Am G Am
think a - bout_ our world to - day.
G Am G Am
3.
D.S. al Coda
G Am G G/B B♭dim7
- day. We have
CODA
G Am Gmaj7 Am G Am G
- day.

TURN OFF THE TAP!

Words and Music by
Niki Davies

Gm7
C7
slop in - to the sink,
have a lit - tle
F
G11
F/A
Gm7
F
G11
think.
1 – 5.
6.
F/A
Gm7
F/C
C7
F
2-5. When you've

USE IT AGAIN

Words and Music by
Niki Davies

F F/A F7/C B♭ B♭m6
- gain. Don't throw it in the bin, you don't
F/C G7 C F/C C
need to put it in, use it a - gain, use it a -
1. 2. 3.
4.
F C B♭/C F C7 F C7 F
- gain. 2. 3. 4. Use it a - - gain.

TURN OFF THE TAP!

1 When you've cleaned your teeth, turn off the tap.
Don't let it go drip, drop,
Slip, slop into the sink,
Have a little think.

2 When you've washed your face, turn off the tap.
Don't let it go drip, drop,
Slip, slop into the sink,
Have a little think.

3 When you've washed your hands, turn off the tap.
Don't let it go drip, drop,
Slip, slop into the sink,
Have a little think.

4 When you've scrubbed your nails, turn off the tap.
Don't let it go drip, drop,
Slip, slop into the sink,
Have a little think.

5 When you've had a drink, turn off the tap.
Don't let it go drip, drop,
Slip, slop into the sink,
Have a little think.

Words and Music by Niki Davies

CCLI Song No. 5184909

Use It Again

1 Use it again, use it again,
If you've got a carrier bag, use it again.
Don't throw it in the bin, you don't need to put it in,
Use it again, use it again.

2 Use it again, use it again,
If you've got a water bottle, use it again.
Don't throw it in the bin, you don't need to put it in,
Use it again, use it again.

3 Use it again, use it again,
If you've got an envelope, use it again.
Don't throw it in the bin, you don't need to put it in,
Use it again, use it again.

4 Use it again, use it again,
If you've got a glass jar, use it again.
Don't throw it in the bin, you don't need to put it in,
Use it again, use it again.

Words and Music by Niki Davies

CCLI Song No. 5184916

PERFORMANCE LICENCE APPLICATION FORM

(EDDIE THE PENGUIN SAVES THE WORLD!)

If you perform ***Eddie The Penguin Saves The World!*** to an audience other than children and staff you will need a performance licence. If you have already purchased an instant performance licence then you do not need to do anything else. If you do not have a current performance licence then you can purchase one online at www.outoftheark.com. Alternatively you can photocopy and complete this form and return it by post or fax to Out of the Ark Music. If anticipated audience sizes are very small or if special circumstances apply please contact Out of the Ark Music.

The performance licence will permit the holder to:

- Perform *Eddie The Penguin Saves The World!* during the licence period.
- Play the audio CD (either the backing or vocal tracks) at the performance(s).
- Reproduce the lyrics to the songs on printed paper, such as for programmes, and project the lyrics or display the lyrics electronically. The following credit should be included:
  'Reproduced by kind permission © Out of the Ark Ltd'.
- Photocopy the script for learning purposes. Copies must be destroyed after the performance.*
- Make no more than two copies of the music, to be used by participating musicians on the performance dates.*
- If you purchase a performance licence online you may also install your Words On Screen™ CD ROM onto your network server or onto two or more computers.

* UK state schools should report any copying of the lyrics and music on their Printed Music Licence (PML) returns.

If the performance is to be recorded please contact Out of the Ark Music.

We wish to apply for a licence to perform *Eddie The Penguin Saves The World!* by Niki Davies

Customer number (if known): ....

Name of school / organisation: ....

Name of organiser / producer: ....

Email address of organiser / producer:..

Invoice address: ....

....

Post code: .... **Country:** ....

Telephone number: ....

This licence to perform ***Eddie The Penguin Saves The World!*** will last for 12 months from the date of application and cover any amount of performances within that period.

If applying retrospectively please enter date of first performance: ....

Price of licence: £19.80

Tick one of the three payment options below: (Invoices will be sent with all licences)

☐ Please bill my school/nursery at the above address (UK schools/nurseries only)

☐ I enclose a cheque (Pounds Sterling) for £19.80 payable to Out of the Ark Music

☐ Please charge £19.80 to the following card: (Visa [not Electron], MasterCard & Maestro accepted)

Card No ....

Start Date _ _ / _ _ (MM/YY) Expiry Date _ _ / _ _ (MM/YY) 3 digit security code: _ _ _ (last 3 digits on signature strip)

Address: Out of the Ark Music
Kingsway Business Park
Oldfield Road
Hampton
Middlesex TW12 2HD
United Kingdom

Phone: +44 (0)20 8481 7200
Fax: +44 (0)20 8941 5548
Email: info@outoftheark.com

The licence fees shown on this form are for 2016 and include VAT at 20%. Prices may be subject to revision.

COPYRIGHT & LICENSING - WHAT YOU NEED TO KNOW

The world of copyright and licensing can seem very daunting, particularly because there is an obligation on schools to comply with copyright law. We're here to help you through the process and to keep you legal. The guidelines below explain the most common copyright and licensing issues. For more information visit www.outoftheark.com/licensing.

STAGING THIS MUSICAL

Performing this musical to an audience (other than pupils and staff) requires a performance licence.

** **Please note that your Performing Rights Society (PRS) Licence does NOT cover musicals** **

We issue affordable performance licences to schools, churches and nurseries. Performance licences can be purchased from www.outoftheark.com. Alternatively complete the performance licence application form on page 38 and fax or post it to us.

The performance licence will permit the holder to:

- Perform the musical on the dates applied for.
- Play the audio CD (either the backing or vocal tracks) at the performance(s).
- Reproduce the song lyrics to the songs on printed paper, such as for programmes, and project the lyrics or display the lyrics electronically. The following credit should be included:
  'Reproduced by kind permission © Out of the Ark Ltd'
- Photocopy the script for learning purposes. Copies must be destroyed after the performance.*
- Make no more than two photocopies of the music score for use by participating musicians on the performance dates.*
- If you purchase a performance licence online you may also install your Words On Screen™ CD ROM onto your network server or onto two or more computers.

* UK state schools should report any copying of the lyrics and music on their Printed Music Licence (PML) returns.

PUTTING ON A CONCERT

If you are not staging this musical but are performing any of our songs for the public on school premises (i.e. to anyone other than pupils or staff) then royalty payments become due. Contact Out of the Ark Music directly to obtain a licence. **Please note:** There is no need to obtain a licence from the publisher if your school has an arrangement with the **Performing Rights Society (PRS)** either directly or through the local authority.

MAKING AN AUDIO RECORDING OR A VIDEO OF THE PERFORMANCE

If you wish to make an audio or video recording of your performance of any of our works please visit www.outoftheark.com/licensing for further information or contact MCPS who will issue you with the relevant licence.

SINGING SONGS IN THE CLASSROOM

You are free to use all of the material – including songs and scripts – in the classroom for teaching purposes. If photocopying any part of the book for teaching purposes please record this usage on your school's photocopy log to ensure that you are legally protected.

SINGING SONGS IN AN ASSEMBLY OR IN CHURCH

Songs may be sung in assembly without charge. However, the reproduction of the lyrics and/or musical scores for use in an assembly or a church requires a licence. The following licences from Christian Copyright Licensing Limited (www.ccli.com) permit the photocopying or reproduction of song lyrics or musical scores – for example to create song sheets, overhead transparencies or to display the lyrics or music using any electronic display medium:

For UK schools: A Collective Worship Copyright Licence (CWCL) and a Music Reproduction Licence (CWMRL)
For churches: A Church Copyright (CCL) and Music Reproduction Licence (MRL)

Please ensure that you log the songs that are used on your CWCL and CWMRL copy report.

Organisations that do not hold one of the above licences should contact Out of the Ark Limited directly for permission.

Your CWCL licence also grants you permission to display the song lyrics from our Words on Screen™ CD ROM on a interactive whiteboard or other type of screen. Simply log the song titles on your copy report.

COPYING AND FILE-SHARING

Copying Out of the Ark Music's audio CDs is not permitted without obtaining a licence from the publisher. Installation of Out of the Ark Music's audio CD tracks on to a computer is strictly forbidden without a licence – we can provide schools with a 'Learning Platform Installation Licence'. File-sharing of any of our audio tracks or CD ROM files is strictly prohibited. For more information visit **www.outoftheark.com/licensing**.

Helpful information can be found on the following website: **A Guide to Licensing Copyright in Schools: www.outoftheark.com/licensing**

And remember, we are always happy to help. For advice simply contact our customer services team:

Tel: +44 (0)20 8481 7200
Email: copyright@outoftheark.com

the Song & Story series
Traditional Stories brought wonderfully to life!
The Gingerbread Man
Rapunzel
The Musicians of Bremen
The Three Little Pigs
Goldilocks and the Three Bears
Chicken Licken
Hansel and Gretel
The Princess and the Pea
The Enormous Turnip
3-6s
Jack and the Beanstalk
The Song & Story Series
by Niki Davies
The Three Billy Goats Gruff
Little Red RidingHood
Far more than just a songbook, this series has been written for use in nurseries, reception and at home.
Traditional, well loved stories re-told through a very simple script and just a few bite-size songs.
Out of the Ark Music